Book 1

Android Crash Course

By: PG WIZARD BOOKS

&

Book 2

XML Crash Course

By: PG WIZARD BOOKS

Book 1

Android Crash Course

By: PG WIZARD BOOKS

Step by Step Guide To Mastering Android Programming!

Android Crash Course: Step by Step Guide To Mastering Android
Programming!

Table of Contents

Introduction

Working with the Android operating system can be a great experience. Unlike some of the other coding languages and operating systems out there, Android is the language that you will work with for mobile devices rather than for your computer. With that being said, you are still able to work on the computer, using an emulator, so that you can check out if the app that you create is going to work properly or not.

If you are interested in creating some of your own apps with the help of the Android operating system, this is the guidebook that is going to help you to get it done. It is a simple program to learn how to use, and this guidebook is going to make it easier than ever to get started. We will talk about some of the basics of working with the Android operating system as well as how it is all set up for you to use. Once that is done, we are going to learn how to download the Android operating system, set up the emulator, write your first code, and even make some changes to it later on. There is so much that you are able to do with the help of this operating system and we are going to take a look at some of the best parts of it with this guidebook.

When you are ready to learn a new coding language for your mobile devices, and you want to be able to create some of your own applications, make sure to check out this guidebook for the basics on how to get started from doing updates, to installing the software and even creating some of your first programs.

Chapter 1: An Overview of Android

If you are someone who likes to work in programming and even on smartphones,
then the Android operating system is a great option for you to use. Android is an
operating system that is based off Linux, which makes it really easy for you to
use. The user interface is considered as direct manipulation based and it is one
that will be used and designed to work with tablets and smartphones that are
touchscreens as well as cars, televisions, and wristwatches that are compatible
with this technology. With the operating system, you are able to make use of the
touch inputs which will be able to correspond with actions that are done in the
real world, such as pinching, swiping, and tapping.

With all of the things that Android is able to work with, you are going to find
many different projects that you are able to create. Android is a really low-cost
operating system that is ready made and can be customized to the needs that you
have. And since it is able to be used with other high-tech devices, it has become
really popular with a wide range of technology companies. Add in that this is an
open source operating system (which means that programmers are able to use it
and make changes as they see fit), it is easy to use on your own projects, and you
can even find a large community of developers who can help you out.

There are many features that you are going to find with the Android system. You
will be able to use it with other languages to work on your device, it has the power
that you need to compete with the Apple operating system and Windows 8.1 it is
able to store all the information that you need, works with your Wi-Fi, and even
has an interface that is intuitive for the user. These are some of the features that
you can enjoy while using the Android operating system and with the new
innovations that are always coming out thanks to this code being open sourced,
you are sure to find other benefits that will help you to get your projects done.

Android is one of the best-operating systems out there for devices like tablets,
televisions, and mobile phones. There are billions of these devices hooked up to
the Android system, and it has quickly become one of the largest mobile platform
bases with a huge growth potential in the future. In fact, according to the Google
Corporation, it is believed that more than a million new devices are activated with
Android each day.

Android Crash Course: Step by Step Guide To Mastering Android Programming!

The interface

By default, the user interface in Android is going to be base don the touch inputs of the user with options like pinching, swiping, and tapping on the objects, or the keyboard on the screen of the device. So basically this is an operating system that is designed to respond to the input of the user right away, and it includes a smooth touch interface to make things easier. You will also find that this operating system is going to put to use the vibration feature of the device, so the user is able to get some haptic feedback.

The internal hardware that comes with this operating system, such as accelerometers, gyroscopes, and proximity sensors are used by the applications, and you can use it for adjusting the orientation of the screen, using remote controls, and even change up the home screen for the different pages that you use. Basically, this is a very intuitive interface that the user is going to love because it responds to their touches and it has so many different options that they are able to use.

Managing the memory

For the most part, the devices that run on Android are going to use battery. So if you want to make sure that the battery life is going to last longer, you will want to have a RAM that will consume less power because they will not get a continuous source of power like some of your desktop devices. Whenever the app is minimized, or it isn't in use, it is going to be placed inside the memory automatically. Yes, these applications are going to be open still, but this method is going to help to prevent it from consuming all the resources of the system; they will simply wait in the background until you decide to call them back up.

This is great for the Android device because you will be able to call it back up as needed, but it helps to save the limited RAM that you have. The RAM is limited because you want to make sure that it doesn't waste out all the battery power that you have this device. Luckily, this system is going to be good at managing some of your applications. If it notices that your memory is running low, it is simply going to terminate the processes that aren't being used, closing up the oldest applications first to save room.

Security and privacy

Many people are worried about getting on a new operating system is whether it is going to keep your privacy safe and if it is secure enough to work on the apps with. There are many operating systems that promise to be amazing when it comes to your security and privacy, but some of them may fall short at some times and won't provide the benefits that you are looking for. But when it comes to the Android operating system, you are going to get all the benefits of a lot of security and privacy, simply by the way that the system is set up to deal with the work that you are doing and since you get to determine how all the apps interact on the computer and get to give each of them permission before they get any information, you know that your privacy is always going to be safe.

The applications that you use in Android are going to run inside the sandbox, which is basically an area of your system that is isolated and will not have access to the other resources unless you give permission for this when you install the application. Before you install a new application, you will also need to give permission in order to get it on the system. This is going to take a bit more time through the installation process, but it helps to prevent bugs in the applications, limits documentation, and helps to keep your information secure and private no matter what.

Works with different languages

One of the nice things about working with the Android operating system is that it is able to work with many other coding languages. Almost all of the major coding languages are supported on these devices, and the list is currently at over 100 languages. This makes it easy for the Android device to adapt to what you want to use. It also supports Java so that if you want to create something to work online, the Java language is going to be easy to use.

These are just some of the things that you are going to fall in love with when you get started on the Android platform. It is great to work with mobile devices, no matter what kind you have, it has a lot of speed and stability so that you know that your coding will work out well, and you can develop many different kinds of applications, in many different coding languages if you want, without too much hassle.

The benefits of working with the Android operating system

Android Crash Course: Step by Step Guide To Mastering Android
Programming!

When it comes to working with an operating system that works out well with your mobile devices, none of them are going to be as great as the Android operating system. There are other options, but the Android operating system is going to work on billions of devices all over the world. Some of the benefits that you will be able to enjoy with this operating system include:

- Easy to use: working with the Android operating system can be really easy. You are going to learn how to create some of your own apps in no time, and then you can bring out your own creativity to work with Android or to create the apps that you dream about.
- Works well with mobile devices: the whole idea of using the Android operating system is so that you are able to use it to create apps that are good for your mobile devices. This can include things like televisions, tablets, and smartphones. You can use the emulator that is available for your computer, or your own device, in order to create an app and then have a chance to try it out to see if it works.
- Works with the Java language: you will need to know how to work with the Java language if you want to work on an Android app. This is a basic website and online building language that is easy to use, but it is important that you learn how to use this ahead of time.
- Allows you to create and sell your own apps: one of the reasons that a lot of people will choose to go with the Android operating system is because they have some ideas for apps that they want to use and hope to sell. There are millions of people who use the Android operating system on their devices, and they are always looking for new apps and games to work with. Some people choose to sell the apps for free, and others will make money off of the added space they sell or the cost of the app. This is a great way to make some extra money if you like to work with apps.
- The user interface is easy to work with: this user interface is meant to be really interactive. In fact, it is going to work mainly by the user working with their hands and fingers rather than relying on buttons and clicks like the other operating systems that you may be used to. This can make it easier for you to learn how to make apps that the customer will love because they can work on it in real time without all the extras going on around it causing it to be slower.
- A big community to ask questions with: the Android system has a big community of people you are able to meet with, ask questions of, and so much more when you need help. Android has been around for a long time,

and it has a lot of devices that will use this system to get things done. This makes it easier for you to use the operating system and to get it to work the way that you would like.

There are many options that you can choose when it comes to making a mobile operating system work for your app. Some people will use the Windows system and other times you will want to go with the Apple iOS. But none have the wide range and all the flexibility that you need from the Android operating system, and this is why so many people choose to go with it. With billions of devices that use this operating system and a million more being added each day, it is no wonder that people love being able to use and learn how to use Android.

Chapter 2: The Architecture of the Android Operating System

Before we get too far into developing our programs with the Android operating system, it is important to know some of the architecture that comes with this program and where things will work together. The framework of the application is easier to understand if we know how things are going to be arranged and will work inside of the operating systems. Since this is an operating system that is based on Linux, you will see that the two are very similar if you have worked with Linux in the past. For those who have never worked on Linux at all, you will notice that the layout of the language is pretty simple to use and you will catch on pretty quickly. Let's take a look at the architecture of this operating system.

Basic applications

The first applications that you are going to see are the basic ones. These are some of the options like the application to make calls, for your music player and camera and more. They don't have to come from Google, and sometimes Google isn't going to provide them at all, but you will be able to use the Google play store in order to develop these kinds of applications and make it so that they are available for everyone to use. You can also develop the apps with Java and then install them into the device that will integrate with the Android operating system.

Application framework

This is the part of the system that is going to be used for developing the applications. This framework is available with many different interfaces, and the developers will pick out which interface they want to use based on the standards that are important to them. By using these frameworks, you are going to save a lot of time and effort because it is not necessary to code out all of the tasks. There are also some different entities that come with the framework, and the options available are going to change based on the framework that you want to use.

Activity manager

Android Crash Course: Step by Step Guide To Mastering Android
Programming!

When you are using the activity manager, you are using the part of the program that is responsible for managing the different activities that control the app life cycle. It is going to have many different states, and the activity manager will be able to handle all of these. The applications are going to consist of many different types of activities, and each of these activities is going to have its own life cycle. Whenever you launch up a new application, one main activity is going to be started. You will be able to pull up a window when needed in order to see every activity inside an app.

Resource managers

If you have some applications that are going to require some kind of external resources, such as an external string, these are going to be managed with the help of your resource manager. These parts are going to be able to allocate the resources in the way that is standard for your device and will make sure that everything works together well.

Libraries

There are several libraries that you are able to us in Android in order to make sure that you are using the right codes, to save time, and to make your work more powerful. All of the native libraries for Android are going to be found inside of this layer, but all of them are going to be written using either the C++ or the C language. The capabilities that are found inside these libraries are going to be similar to what you find in the application layer on the top of the Linux kernel. Some of the things that you are going to find inside of these libraries on Android will include:

- Surface manager: this is the compositing window in manager and display.
- System C libraries: these are the basic libraries of C that are going to be targeted for the ARM or embedded devices.
- A media framework: this could include options for playback, recording, video, audio, and more.
- OpenGL ES libraries: this is the one that is needed for the graphics on the device.

12

- SQLite: this is a database engine. This one, in particular, is a smaller version that works better on Android without using up as much memory space.

All of these are going to come together in order to help you to find out the codes that you would like to use inside your program. You can use these as a simple way to get started on the app that you would like to use or as some suggestions as to what you would need to do next. You can always add in some of the other parts that you would like if the code really needs it, but this is one of the best places to start as a beginner in order to get your basics down and to start writing some of your own code.

Android Runtime

You will find that the Dalvik Virtual Machine is the part that is in charge of the runtime for all Android devices. This is a virtual machine that is going to be used for your embedded devices as well as an interpreter for bytecode. They are going to have lower memories and can be a bit slower than you are used to since they run on batteries. You will find that the Java libraries are also going to be on these devices which means that you will be able to use them.

Kernel

When it comes to using the Android operating system, you will be using the Linux Kernel 2.6. This is going to include all the electronic equipment that you need, and many of the processes are going to be similar to what you will find with the Linux operating system to make things easier. Between the software and hardware of Android, you are going to see that the kernel will behave similar to the abstraction layer in the hardware and will include essential parts like the keypad, camera, and display. The kernel is also going to be in charge of handling things like the networking and device drivers.

Keep in mind that working with the Linux system means that everything is going to be in the form of a kernel. This helps to add in some security to the system and makes the whole program easier to use. If you have ever worked with the Linux system, you are used to how easy the Linux operating system is to do a lot of different tasks, and this is going to translate over to the work that you are doing over on the Android operating system as well.

Android Crash Course: Step by Step Guide To Mastering Android
Programming!

Now that you know a bit more about the different parts that come with the
Android operating system and how it does work quite well with the Linux system,
it is time to move on to downloading this software properly and working on a few
of your very first projects to make things easier.

Chapter 3: Working on Your First Project

Now that we have taken the time to learn more about the Android system, it is time to work on our first project. This one is going to be pretty simple to learn, but will help you to get a feel for how all of this works for some of the other topics we will bring up later on. But the first step that we need to take when getting started is to install the Android Studio.

To start with this, we need to see if the Java Development Kit, or the JDK, is installed on your computer or not. Some computers come with this already in place so that can save you time. For a PC, you need to click on Start, Run, type in the word "cmd" and then press enter to see if it is there. If you are on a Mac computer, you will use the Spotlight to search for the Terminal and then choose the top result. If this is on the computer, use the prompt "java-version." If a command is not found, you will need to visit the Oracle website and download the JDK on your computer.

Once this is done, it is time to go online and download the right version of the Android Studio for your computer. When this has had time to download the right way on the computer, you can click on Next to move on to the following screen. At this location, you will need to pick the setup that you want to use (standard is usually the best one) before clicking on Next and accepting the license agreements. At this point, the Android Studio is going to finish up the download, and you are ready.

For each version of Android that you are using, you will find that it contains a version of SDK for you to work with. The setup wizard is going to help you to get the updated versions of this. It is important to have the SDK because it helps you to set up the Android Virtual Device, the part that allows you to test your new apps on it and you can give it the right customizations for your own personal configuration.

So go back to the Welcome Screen of the Android Studio and click Configure. You should see a new menu that offers you a lot of options, and you will want to pick the one that says SDK Manager. A new window should appear when you click on this, and a series of folders, checkboxes, and statuses are going to show up. If you just downloaded the Android Studio, you should have the latest version of SDK

Tools as well as some of the other tools to make the program work. If you see that
an update is still available for this, the box will be ticked, and you can choose
whether or not you want to take this.

Once you have had time to get the latest version of the SDK Manager on your
computer (taking the time to update it if you need), it is time to create one of your
first programs inside of the Android operating system.

Creating the OMG Android

Now it is time to start working on your very first project, and we are going to start
out pretty simple, using the Hello, World! Kind of idea that the other coding
languages go with. The idea behind this one is to give you some options and
familiarity with using Android so that you can do some of the bigger projects later
on.

The nice thing that you will notice about the Android Studio is that it comes with
a nice tool that will give you the steps that you need to get this project started.
You will just need to get on the Welcome Screen, click that you want to start a
New Android Studio Project, and then the screen for project creation will show
up. You are allowed to place an application name, and we are going to call this
one OMG Android. For the company domain just put in your name. You may
notice that the Package Name is going to change at this time to make a reverse
domain name based on what you call the application and your company. This is
going to be like a unique identifier so that the app is easily found among all the
others.

Set the project location to the hard drive location that you would like before
clicking on Next. On this screen, you are going to tell the system which devices
and operating systems you would like to make the app work with. You probably
don't want to make an app that will work with each Android device, but you can
narrow this down to just smartphones or just tablets if you would like. For this
one, to keep things easier, we are going to target the Android phone (you should
see that this is the default option selected along with the Minimum SDK).

You can then click on Next to get to the following screen to choose what activity
will happen for the app. A good way to think about this is as a window inside the

16

app that will be able to show what content will be interactive with the user. You can use this activity as a popup or as the while window. Inside of this template, the activities are going to range from being blank with an Action Bar all the way to one that has an embedded Map View. But for this project, we are going to keep things simple and work with Blank Activity before clicking Next.

At this point, you are almost to the coding. We are going to go through and use the default options with this and then click on the Finish button. There will be a few minutes for the Studio to go through and finish off the project and sometimes you will notice that it is going through all the different steps and putting out information about what it is doing. The nice thing is that with this IDE, a lot of work is going to be done for you.

After a few minutes, the Studio is going to finish building up this project. This project so far is going to be empty since we didn't put in any code to it, but it will contain all the information that is needed to be launched on one of the Android devices. At this point, you should see that there are three windows that are open on the Android Studio. On the left is going to be the project folder, the middle will have a preview of what this looks like on the Nexus 5, and then the last window is going to show the layout of the project.

Right now the project is pretty empty and will not show much up on the screen, but you will be able to make changes to that later on and add in some words as well as some other really cool things. But for now, you have created a good program so let's take that a step further in the next chapter and not only add in some of the words or phrases that you need to work with inside this operating system, but also learn how to make the app run with your emulator or with the Android   device.

Chapter 4: Running the App

So in the last chapter, we spent some time making a pretty basic app. We learned
how to get it all setup and that the Android Studio is really great at setting the
defaults that you want to use and which will ensure that you have it named the
right way and ready to go. But so far the app doesn't have any words in it for
others to see or any other actions, and it isn't running in a way that the other
Android apps will be able to use. This chapter is going to take some time to add in
these two options so that you can make your app start to work.

Running the app on an Emulator

So with the example that we did in the previous chapter, we took the time to
create our first app, but now we need to figure out how to run that. If you already
own an Android device, you are able to use this to run and test out the app, but if
you don't have a device, you can choose to work with an emulator. The Android
Studio is going to include the abilities that you need to set up a software-based
device right on your computer. This basically means that you can run apps, debut
the app, and look through a website on your computer, but it will work as if you
were on the Android app. You will be able to set up as many emulators on your
computer, and you can mess around with the screen size, version of the platform,
and more to really see how the app is going to work.

If you went through the setup wizard properly on the last steps, you could already
have the emulator in place on your computer. But we are going to take a moment
to set up a brand new emulator in case you missed this option before or if you
would like to choose a second emulator on the computer.

To get started on this is to click on the AVD Manager. You should be able to look
inside of the toolbar for the icon that has the Android popping up and is beside a
device with a purple display. The Android Studio is going to have one of these
setups that you are able to use, and you will be able to see some details about the
type of the emulator, the API that it uses, and the CPU instructions.

But if you would like to create a brand new AVD, you will just need to click on the
Create Virtual Device. Now you will need to come up with some choices. For the
first one, you will need to decide which device you would like to emulate. You
should be able to look over to the left and see a list of categories that basically list
all of the devices that you will be able to emulate and then you can see the
different devices in each category. To make things simple, we are going to click on
the Phone category and choose the Nexus S. once you pick this one, click on the
Next.

Now you also need to decide on the Android version you would like to use. There
are a few options that are available, and we are going to pick one of them,
Lollipop. Check that when you are on this that the ABI column shows a value of
x86 to ensure that the emulator is going to run at a good speed. Click on the Next
button. This page should basically be a confirmation screen that you should
double check before clicking on Finish and ending this process.

At this point, you have created a brand new virtual device that will allow you to
test out your app. You should close down the AVD Manager and then head back
to your main screen of the Android Studio. For the final step, you will click on
Run before another window shows up and you can choose which device you want
to test this app on. You shouldn't have any of the devices running here so you can
start with the AVD that you created earlier, just make sure to click on the Launch
Emulator and that the AVD is selected before clicking on OK.

Here you will need to give the emulator some time to load up, and you may even
need to do this a few times to get it right. Once all of this is loaded properly, you
will be able to see what there is of the running app.

So now that this emulator is all set up, it is time to add a bit more to the code that
we did earlier so that we can see how it is going to work on other Android devices.
We are going to keep this one simple right now, but you can always expand on
this to get more out of it. So to start on this, you will need to go to
res/values/strings.xml and then double click on this file. We are going to change
this so that we can make it a bit more personal and have some fun with it. Here is
the syntax of what you should type in:

<string name = "hello_world">I am learning Android!

</string>

Android Crash Course: Step by Step Guide To Mastering Android
Programming!

You would be able to change up the code to say anything that you would like
inside of this part of the code, making the string a lot longer, changing up the
message, and so much more. This is just a great little way of showing how the
code can work. But with this one, you have created your first app and even made
some changes to make it a bit more personalized. You will just need to click on
Run when it is done, and the message that you wrote out should show up on the
screen.

Chapter 5: Doing Updates with the SDK Manager

Now we are going to take some time to do a bit more with the app that you want to create. This is all going to work regardless of the version of SDK that you would download on your computer so even if one of the older versions is there; it will still work. If you would like to make sure to open up the SDK Manager from inside the project, you will just need to click on the button that has the downward arrow with your Android peeking above it. When we are done with this section, we are going to be able to make a lot of changes to the app, and we will have one that has a PNG image, has an editable text field, and so much more.

So at this point, we need to have our "Hello, World!" app open and ready to go on the device, or you can use the emulator if that is the method that you would like to work with so that the message is showing. But now it is time to take this over to the next level.

Getting started on this project

For this one, we are going to take a moment to look ahead. The first thing that you will want to do with this step of the project is to make sure that the app is going to be simple. You don't want to add in a lot of complexities at this part because this can slow down the app, introduces some more bugs to the system, and just makes it more difficult for the user to work with. You only want to add in extra parts if you really need it for the app to work properly, but right now this is going to take some more time and work than what we want to work with at the time.

So to get started, we are going to need to open up the app/res/layout/activity_main.xml. If you are able to see the .raw and .xml file, you will be good to go. But if this is not showing up, you will need to go to the bottom of your screen and see if you need to switch all of this over to the Text mode. All we will do at this point is work to get rid of some of the attributes that are just padding to it. The Studio often adds these things to the .xml file on its own, but it can make it harder to work on the file. You are going to want to look for and delete all of these lines before we continue:

android:paddingLeft="@dimen/activity_horizontal_margin

android:paddingRight=@dimen/activity_horizontal_margin

android:paddingTop=@dimen/activity_vertical_margin

android:paddingBottom=@dimen/activity_vertical_margin

If you went through all of this and did it the proper way, your new .xml file is going to look like the following:

<RelativeLayout

xmlns:android=http://schemas.android.com/apk/res/android

xmlns:tools=http://schemas.android.com/tools

android:layout_width="match_parent"

android:layout_height="match_parent"

tools:context=".MainActivity">

<TextView

android:text="@string/hello_world

android:layout_width="wrap_content"

android:layout_height="wrap_content"/>

</RelativeLayout>

At this point, we will need to look for the Mainactivity.java part of the code. You will need to look on the left pane that is inside of Studio and then double click on it. We are going to take a moment to look at the very first piece of code, and you will need to move out a few of the lines including the following:

@Override

public boolean onOptionsItemSelected(MenuItem item){

```
//Handle action bar item clicks here. The action bar will

//automatically handle clicks on the Home/Up button, so long

//as you specify a parent activity in AndroidManifest.xml.

int id = item.getItemId();


//noinspection SimplifiableIfStatement

if (id == R.id.action_settings){

return true;

}


return super.onOptionsItemSelected(item);

}
```

You should be careful when you are doing this to make sure that you are leaving the final curly brace in its place when you delete the other options. This is the curly brace that is going to close up your class ahead of it, and you want to make sure that it is still there. Now that all the housekeeping work has been done, it is time to get to work and give the Activity a new life of its own.

Chapter 6: How to Publish Your Android App

Now that we have had some time to create our own app a little bit and learn how to manage the app in a way that makes it have less stuff in the way and so that it does more of the work that you want, it is time to learn how to publish your own app. You are going to work with making a lot of different types of apps over the years when you get familiar with working with the Android operating system and it is likely that you will at some point want to be able to publish one of the apps to make some money or for other people to be able to use it as well. In this chapter, we are going to spend some time learning how to take one of the apps that you create and getting it published.

The first thing to know is that when creating an Android app, you will need to publish it on the Google Play store. This means that you will need to create your own account using the Google Play Developer Console. This account is going to cost a little bit of money to create, about $25 at the publishing of this book, but considering the other parts of the operating system are free, this isn't so bad. The reason that there are fees with this account is that the Google company wants to keep out people who would make duplicate or fake accounts and helps to avoid people flooding the store with bad apps that no one else wants.

After you have gone through and created the account and paid the beginning fees, you are going to have your own Google Play Developer Account. You will be able to choose as many apps as you would like to publish on this account and you can choose whether you would like to publish those apps for free for others to use or in a manner to make money through the system. Some people are turned away by the fees, but if you are looking to make some money with this system on your apps by selling them, you will find that you can quickly make this $25 back. You can also allow ads to be on your app and earn some ad-revenue if you would like.

So to get this started, you just need to visit the site https://developer.android.com/distribute/index.html. Then you will just need to follow the steps that come up on the prompts to help you figure out what you are supposed to do to finish the account. In the end, you will finish creating your own developer account, pay the fees that are associated with the account to get it started, and then complete the process.

At this point, you are probably done with creating your append are ready to
upload it into the system. You will just need to upload the app file in a manner
that is similar to how you would attach a link or a document into your email.
Then you will be asked to take a survey. This is not something that you will be
able to skip out on because the system wants to know about the different factors
and features about your app. Some of the questions that it is going to ask is about
whether there are inappropriate contents inside and if there are any age
restrictions on using the app.

After you are done with setting up your account and getting the app to upload
inside of the program, you are going to need to give Google a few days in order to
validate the app. You will be able to add in as many of these apps as you would
like over time, but you still need to give it a few days before it is going to show up
inside the app store.

And that is all that you would need to do in order to get the app to work inside of
the Google Play Store. You will be able to choose to offer the game for free, add
some ad revenue into the system to make money, or charge for people to use the
app in the first place. There are many options about the type of apps that you are
able to use, and since it is so easy to add it to the Google store, you will be able to
develop the app, get it put up, and move on to the next project in no time.

Conclusion

The Android operating system is a great one for you to learn how to use whenever you are looking to create an app or another program that works on phones, tablets, televisions and other mobile options. It is based on the Linux system which makes it easy to learn how to use (especially if you already know how to use this system), and you will find that over 100 coding languages are recognized on Android, so you are able to pick the one that is best for you.

In this guidebook, we took some time to look at the different parts of the Android operating system. We started out with some of the basics of this system before moving on to how set up the architecture that is inside of the code, how to create one of your own programs, and even how to set up an emulator so that you can run the code on your computer (which can be nice if you don't have a specific Android device around) and see how it is going to work for you.

There is so much to love with the Android operating system. With billions of devices around the world using this system for making apps or running the programs that they want on their mobile devices, it is easy to learn how to use this operating system for developing your own apps or for your own personal use. Use this guidebook to learn more about how the Android operating system works and to make it create the best programs for you.

Book 2

XML Crash Course

By: PG WIZARD BOOKS

Step by Step Guide To Mastering XML Programming!

XML Crash Course: Step by Step Guide To Mastering XML Programming!

Table of Contents

Introduction

When it comes to getting into the world of coding and all the programming that you would like to do, there are many options that you are able to choose from. Some choose to work with options like Java and HTML so that they can create projects online and on web pages that really wow. Others like to go with Python because it is an easy one for beginners to work with. But a great coding language that you can learn to work with and which we are going to discuss inside this guidebook, is the XML coding language.

You will notice as you go through this guidebook that there are some similarities that come up between the XML language and the HTML language. While both of these are similar, there are some differences that come up and we will talk about these inside of this guidebook. We will also spend some time talking about some of the basics of XML, some of the parts that you would want to add into the code to make things easier, how to declare XML documents (which is something optional you are able to do to make the code work a bit better) and even how to work with the different character entities to help make coding easier. These are just a few of the things that we will discuss in order to get you familiar with the XML code so that you can use it on your own.

When you are ready to get started on a new coding language and you want to pick one of the very best that is also easy for beginners to work with, you should learn how to use XML. This guidebook is going to give you the best results to ensure that you will learn everything that you need to know in order to start with the XML language.

Chapter 1: What is XML Programming?

When it comes to learning a new programming language, there are so many choices and it can all seem a bit overwhelming. You want to make sure that you are picking choices that will get you ahead and will make it easier to work on the systems and programs that you want, but with all of the choices that are out there, how are you going to be able to choose the one that is right for you. There are choices for beginners and ones for those who want to be a bit more advanced. There are choices that are great for working on websites while others are good for a specific operating system or for working inside of your business statistics. There really isn't a right or wrong answer, you just need to take the time to look at the different options and find the one that is right for you.

In this guidebook, we are going to take a look at the XML program. This one stands for Extensible Markup Language and it is one of the most talked about programming languages, only second to Java, because of all the great things that you are able to work with. inside of this language, you are able to store, organize, and identify your information with the help of tags. If you have used Java or JavaScript programming in the past, you may have heard about HTML tags, but these two are not quite the same. The XML language is not one that is going to replace HTML later on down the road, but it does introduce some new possibilities because it uses some of the features of HTML.

So, to make this easy, the XML program is going to be software and hardware independent and it is often used in order to carry information. even though the markup that is used will look similar to what you are finding with HTML, you will see that these are two different entities. For example, XML is set up to focus on the data that you are using while HTML is more focused on the appearance of your data. XML is going to describe your data while the HTML is going to display the data when you are done.

To make this work better, let's take a look at a good example of how this will work. Keep in mind that you will need to define some of your own tags because these are not predefined inside of XML. Here is the example:

<note>

```
<to>Jane</to>

<from<John</from>

<heading>Memo</heading>
```

<body>Come to the meeting at ten in the morning tomorrow</body>

</note>

With this example, you are probably able to tell what is going on. The information is there for both the sender as well as the receiver and there are headings and a body message that you will be able to use. But remember that the XML document is basically going to contain the information that you want along with some tags. There are no specific functions that go with it. On its own, XML is going to be pretty useless until you get the right software program in there to turn it into something.

Now basically, you are going to have three characteristics that come with the XML language that you are able to use and you can remember these by thinking about the name of the program. The three characteristics that you can work with include:

Extensible: this means that the XML program is going to allow you the change to characterize your own tags so that they will work with your application. You will also be able to extend the concept of the document, which is usually a file that is going to live on the server. It can also be a piece of data that is temporary and will flow between the various web servers.

Markup: this it eh elements or the tags that are familiar inside of XML. The elements that you are creating in this language will be similar to the ones in HTML, but you will be able to define the elements or tags that you want.

Language: the languages that are used inside of HTML and XML are pretty similar, but there is some more flexibility when using XML. You are able to use it to create and define some other languages rather than just having it set in stone like HTML.

Do I really need to learn how to use XML?

XML Crash Course: Step by Step Guide To Mastering XML Programming!

Many people wonder if it is worth their time to learn how to use XML since it is so similar to what you will find in HTML. You do need XML because there are times when you would like to create and deal with the data. The HTML document is just going to display the information; it is not going to work with it to make it look nicer or anything else.

In addition, working with XML allows you to use different contexts that are not just found on the web, including applications and web services. Any time that you would like to organize your data and send it over to another person, without having to worry about all the displays like you would find with HTML, the XML language is going to be the one to work with.

Downloading the XML language

Before we go any further in this guidebook and learn how to write some codes (as well as some of the other cool things that you are able to do in this language), we are going to need to take some time to get all of this downloaded onto the computer. The XML language is from Microsoft and at the time of this book, the XML Parser 3.0 is the option that we are going to use for our projects.

First, you need to make sure that the operating system and computer are the right kind to run this. To work with the XML Parser 3.0, you will need to have a Windows computer that is Windows 2000, Windows Server 2003, or Windows XP. You can then go to the Microsoft website to find this version, or a newer version, of the XML program an download it to your computer. Read through the prompts that come up on your screen until you get don with the download and it is all installed on your computer. At this point, you are ready to get started with some coding!

Chapter 2: Learning the Basic Syntax of XML

Now that we have the right program on our computer and ready to go, it is time to learn a bit about the syntax of a code in XML. If you learn the basic syntax of your code, it is going to be much easier to write more complex codes later on. Of course, with the options that we are going to talk about in this chapter, we are going to keep things pretty simple to start, but as you learn more about XML, it is pretty easy to add in the other parts that you will want to learn.

Below we are going to write out a basic syntax that you are able to use in this language and then we will take some time to discuss the different parts so that is makes sense for what you are doing. Here is the basic syntax that you can use:

```
<?xmlersio="1.0^)>

<contact-info>

<name>Manny Dunphy</name>

<company>Real Realtor</company>

<phone>(895) 444-1111</phone>

</contact-info>
```

As you can see with this example there are several parts of information that are placed inside. You need to make sure that the right syntax is used and the right symbols, so that the compiler has an idea of what you would like to send. This is a pretty simple option that will have the contact information for this person, Manny Dunphy, who works with Real Realtor as well as their phone number. You can expand this out as much as you would like or keep it this simple.

Remember than when working in XML, we are concentrating on the data, and collecting the data, rather than worrying about how the data is going to look. If you plan on putting this kind of information into a website or you want to make sure that it looks nice, you are going to need to work with the HTML format to make this happen.

XML Crash Course: Step by Step Guide To Mastering XML Programming!

Working with XML declarations

When it comes to XML, there are some documents that are going to have declarations and some that will not. If your document is one of them that has the declaration, here is a good example of how you would want to write it all out:

<?xmlv version="1.0" encoding="UTF-8"?>

For this one, the version is going to be the XML version and the other specific encoding is going to tell the document that you are going to use character encoding for this particular project. As we go through some of the other parts that you are able to work on in this book, you will see some more of the XML declaration and it is going to make a bit more sense to you.

Tags and Elements

Next on the list to work with are the elements and tags. The elements inside of XML are basically going to be the building blocks. They are going to be like a container that will hold many of the different parts of the XML ode, including media objects, attributes, elements, and text. Pretty much any element that comes into the code could be placed into the containers here. Each document is going to contain at least one element, but often there will be more if the code is longer. You can use the scopes in order to delimit using a start or end tag. Here is a good example of how you would write out the syntax for the elements and tags:

<element-name attribute1 attribute2>

...content

</element-name>

The element name in this example is the name that you would give to the element in this place. The name needs to be the same and matching in the beginning as well as in the ending tags. The attribute1 and attribute 2 are the element attributes that are going to be separated by some white space. You will be able to use the attributes in order to refer to a property of the element and often it is going to be associated with not only a name inside the code, but also with a certain value that you assign.

Writing out a comment inside of XML

There are times when you would like to leave a little comment inside of the code. When it comes to coding, the comments are just messages that the compiler is going to skip over and not read, but which can be useful to you or the other programmers who would like to go through the code. You will find that the syntax for writing out comments inside of XML is going to be the same as doing so in HTML. You will be able to use this syntax in order to write out your comment:

<!—An example of a comment→

Comments will need to all be done in this manner to tell the compiler when to start and stop the comment. When the compiler sees this, it will just skip over to the next part of the code, without causing any delays or issues in the code. You are able to add in as many of these comments as you would like or feel that you need in the code to make things easier, but you should be careful to not add in too many or you will end up with a messy code.

Starting a new line inside of XML

There are times when you will want to get started on a new line in XML. When it comes to doing this in applications of Windows, the new line is going to be done with the carriage return and line feed. On the old MAC systems, the new line is going to be with the carriage return and in Unix it is going to be the line feed. But when you are using XML, this is all going to be done with the line feed. You are able to start a new line in the code when you need to keep things in order and to make it easier to read through the code.

Unlike what you are going to find with HTML, the XML code is going to see white spaces a bit different. While you are able to have several whitespaces in a row on HTML, you will not have this inside of XML. Instead, if you have more than one whitespace in a row, the XML program is going to take these and turn them into just one.

XML Crash Course: Step by Step Guide To Mastering XML Programming!

These are just some of the basics that you are able to use when it comes to working in the XML coding language. They are going to help you to form some of the basics of your code and can come in use later on when you are ready to write out some more complicated codes. Make sure to learn some of these basics to make it easier for code writing later on and to further understand how the XML code will work for you.

Chapter 3: Declaring Inside of XML

We discussed the XML declaration a bit earlier on, but now we are going to break this down a bit in order to help it make more sense for you to use. The XML declaration is going consist of the details that you need to put in order by an XML processor to break down and analyze the document of XML. This is an optional feature that you can choose to either use or not use, however, when you do choose to use it, you will notice that it occurs right at the beginning of the document. Here is the syntax that you can use for XML declaration to make things a bit easier to use.

```
<?xml

       Version="version_nmuber"

       Encoding="encoding_delcaration"

       Standalone="standalone_status"

?>
```

Each of the parameters that you are going to use will have their own name so keep these in line and then an equal sign as well as a value. You are able to set up the numbers, rather than the quotes, to get the code to react in the way that you would like. There are a few rules that you will need to keep in mind when you are declaring inside of XML and these rules include the following:

- If there is a declaration inside of XML, you will need to make sure that you position it as the first line in your document. If you put it somewhere else inside of the document, you are going to run into some issues.
- When working with a declaration inside of XML, you will need to have a version number attribute to help make it work.
- The names and the parameter values that you set are going to be case sensitive, and it is recommended that while working inside of XML you keep the names in the lower case.
- There is a proper order that you are going to use with the parameter name to ensure that the compiler will read it properly. The proper order includes

version, encoding, and then standalone, just like you will see with the example that we gave above.

- You get to choose the quote type that you use, either the single or the double quotes. Just make sure that this stays consistent in the code.
- You will also notice that in this declaration, you will not need to have a closing tag like you do in some of the other coding that you will work with.
- If you are doing an encoding declaration, this is going to be a bit different, but for the rest of the declaration, you will need to keep it all in lower case letters.
- If you find that there are attributes, entities, and elements that are referenced or defined by an external DTD, your standalone is going to equal "no".

So now that we know a few of the rules that go with XML declaration, let's take a look at how you would do this in the code to get a better feel for it. This example is going to have all of the parameters defined for us.

```
<?xml> version='1.0' encoding='iso-8859-1' standalone='no'?>
```

And that is all there is to declaring inside of XML. Any time that you would need to do this inside of your code, you can just use this simple syntax, and then add in the information that you would like inside. This makes it easy for you to get the results that you want and as you can see, this only takes up about a line of code (maybe a little more depending on the declaration that you are using) and then you are all set.

Chapter 4: Working with Character Entities and Comments in XML

We talked about comments and some of the characters that you would use in XML a little bit before, but now we need to take this a step further and start to work on how the comments and the characters are going to work when it is time to actually write the code that you would like. When it comes to working with comments inside of XML, you will notice that they are similar to the comments that you have in HTML. They are basically little notes that are added into the code that will help you and other programmers to understand what is going on in the code, but will have absolutely no effect on how the code will work when it runs. One thing to note when writing out a comment is that you shouldn't try to nest one comment inside of another, because this will just cause a mess and could bring up an error inside of the code. Here is an example of a code that would have a comment in it (take the time to write this in your compiler to get some good practice).

```
<?xml version="1.0" encoding="UTF-8"?>
<!—Test scores are uploaded by grade -→
<class_list>
        <student>
        <name>Lilly</name>
        <grade>B+</grade>
        </student>
        </class_list>
```

Of course, this is a pretty simple example that just has one student and it is likely that you would add in a few more to fill this out but it is a good look at how the comment would be able to work inside of the code. It explains that the test scores were going to be upgraded by the grade that you were using and since we only used one it was not the most important, but if you had a lot of other students in here, it would show up. Remember that you are able to add in as many of these comments as you would like, you just need to be careful about using the right symbols to tell the compiler what you are doing.

Character Entities

The entity of the XML document is going to be the root of the entity tree and it is really the starting point for the processor. It can also be seen as the placeholder. The entities are going to be acknowledged being in the document prolog or in the DTD and they will often work with symbols that are only used for the entities and never for the content inside the code. For example, the < and > symbols are only used for the closing and the opening and the character entities are going to be used to make these visible.

Types of character entities

There are a number of character entities that you will be able to use inside of your code including the following:

Predefined character entities

These character entities are going to be introduced in order to prevent the ambiguity that can come when certain symbols are used. For example, there could be some issues when the (<) and (>) symbols are used along with the angle tags of (<>). The character entities are going to help delimit tags. You are able to use some of the following tags in order to get the right results in your code without showing all of the ambiguity at the same time:

Greater than: &gt

Less than: &lt

Ampersand: &amp

Single quote: &apos

Double quote: &wuot

Numerical character entities

With this entity, we are going to use numbers in order to reference and define the character entity that we want to use. We are able to choose numbers that are in decimal and hexadecimal format. There are lots of numeric references that you are able to use, and sometimes there can be too many for you to remember. The numeric reference is a number that is found in the Unicode character set. The syntax that you are going to be able to use for the decimal number reference inside of XML includes:

&# decimal number.

And then when you would like to use the hexadecimal reference, you would go with the following syntax:

&#x Hexadecimal number

Named character references

Wile the numerical character entities are a great way to get started, remember all of these numbers can be really hard, especially as a beginner who is just getting started with coding. This is why most people are going to use the name character entity instead to make things a little easier. There are a number of different ways that you can name the actions that you want to do inside of your code with the name character references, but here are a few of the examples that you can try:

- Acute: this one is going to refer to a capital A character that will have an acute accent on it.
- Ugrave; this is the name of the small u that has a grave accent.

Character entities and types are important when it comes to working inside of your code. They are going to help you to give the assignments to your work, whether you choose to use the numeric or one of the other choices. You can pick out the one that is right for you to work on your XML code.

Chapter 5: Processing and Encoding Inside Your XML Document

In this chapter, we are going to spend some time working on processing and encoding inside of your document. When you choose to work with processing instructions, you are allowing the documents to contain instructions for every application. You should know that these processes and the instructions are not going to be included in the character data that we talked about in the previous chapter, but they will still need to be able to pass through the application that you are creating.

The processing instructions will allow you to pass on the information that you would like to all of the different applications. You are able to place these in any location of the document that you would like. In fact, you are also able to place them into the prolog, which could include the document type definition or DTD, or at the end of the document as the textual content. The syntax to use in order to make this happen includes:

<?target instructions?>

For this syntax, the target is going to be responsible for recognizing the application from which the instruction comes from. You will be able to place the name of any application that you would like to use to tell the program where the instructions are located to use. And then the part of the instructions is going to be used in order to describe any of the information that you would like the application to process in order to finish it out.

The processing instructions are not used all that often because of the specialties that come with it. But if you do choose to work with these processing instructions, you will use them in order to link your XML document to a style sheet. In order to make this happen, you would need to type out the following type of syntax:

<?xml-stylesheet href= "businessforms.css" type="text/css"?>

These are basically the instructions that your target application is going to process inside of the XML document. With this particular instruction, the browser is going to be able to get the browser to recognize the right target by initiating that XML document and that it should transform it before it is shown. Notice that the first attribute comes out as the type of XSL that you are trying to transform and then the second attribute is going to indicate the location of the type you are transforming.

Working with XML encoding

Now that we have talked a bit about using processing inside of the XML document, it is time to work on the encoding inside of your documents. The process of encoding inside of XML is to convert the Unicode characters that you are trying to use into binary ones. The moment that the processor for XML reads a specific document, it is going to immediately encode the document according to the encoding type that you pick to go with it. There are different types of coding that you are able to use and we are going to look at them a bit more below:

Types of encoding

Inside of the XML code, there are gong to be two types of encoding that you are able to use, the UTF-8 and UTF16. They can both be used in separate ways in the coding that you work on. But if you end up not picking out the encoding that you would like to use with your XML document, the default is going to be the UTF-8. The syntax that you are going to use will depend on the type of encoding that you are using. For the UTF-8, you would use the following syntax:

<?xml version="1.0" encoding="UTF-8" standalone="no"?>

And then the syntax that you would need to use for the UTF-16 encoding would include:

<?xml version="1.0" encoding="UTF-16" standalone="no"?>

As you can see, these are going to be pretty similar, you will just put in the different options that you are able to use for the encoding. You will just need to pick the one that is best for you or choose to leave it blank so that the UTF-8 is going to be picked by default. Here is a good example of using the encoding of UTF-8:

```
<?xml version="1.0" encoding="UTF-8" standalone="no"?>
<contact-info>
        <name>Dunny Bobbins</name>
        <company>Real Realtors</company>
        <phone>(553) 512 1123</phone>
</contact-info>
```

With this example, we are using the UTF-8 encoding, as you are able to see by looking at that part of the code. This means that the 8-bit characters are the ones that you will use. For the most part, you would use this option when you want to have files that are encoded to be smaller because you are just going with 8 bits or smaller. If you don't care as much about the size of the file or you would like to get it to be bigger, the UTF-16 is going to be the option that you should use for your encoding.

And that is all there is to the encoding process. It is simple to use and will ensure that the document is going through the right processes to work properly. You can choose to go with either the UTF-8 or the UTF-16 based on your needs, but most of the time the UTF-8 is the best one to choose to go with and if you don't place an option into the code, you are going to find that the processor will choose to go with the UTF-8 by default.

Chapter 6: Working with the Elements and Tags

Earlier we spent some time talking about the elements and tags inside of the XML document, but we are going to now spend a bit more time on this to see how they actually work inside the code and how you can get them to work for your needs. When you are working inside of the XML program, tags are going to be one of the most vital parts. They are the foundation to your language because they are able to do so many things. You will be able to use them as a method to define the scopes of your elements, insert special instructions, declare settings necessary for parsing environments, and to insert comments. There are several different types of tags that you are able to use in XML and they are categorized by this:

Start tag

The start tag is the one that you will use in order to start all of the elements in XML that are non empty. You would be able to write it out similar to this: <address>

Empty tag

Another type of tag that you are going to use is an empty tag. In between the start tag and the end tag (which we are going to talk about soon), is the text that you are going to write out, or the content, of the code. If your element ends up not having any content, you will find that the tag is considered empty. There are a few ways that you are able to represent the empty elements that you are working with.

To start, if you would like to have an end tag that comes right after your start tag, you would just write it out like this "<hr> </hr>". You are also able to have an element tag that is completely empty such as writing out "<hr />". You are able to use these empty element tags for any of the elements inside of the code that aren't going to contain any content inside of them.

The end tag

In addition to the two types of tags that we have been discussing so far, you can also work with the end tag. This is just as necessary as working with the start tag because it tells the code when that particular part is all done or not. You would have a simple syntax to write out in order to make this happen, including </address>. This is going to be the complement to working with the start tag and you will need to have both of these in place inside of the code. Keep in mind that it will need to have the (/) symbol in front of it in order to prevent confusion and to help end out that part of the card.

Some of the rules for using tags in XML

Sometimes it can be a good idea to know the rules about the tags before you get too far into this process. This will help to speed things up and ensure that you are going to get the best results. Unlike some of the other languages that you will work with inside of coding, XML is going to be considered case sensitive. This basically means that you are going to have to take note and be careful when you are using upper case and lower case letters. The tags that you are creating inside of XML will need to be either all upper case letter or all lower case letters. You will find that a simple mistake in this field is going to give you some bad results, so always make sure to review each of the codes that you will use before finalizing them.

For example, if you typed into the code <address> and then ended it as </Address>, the code is going to have some troubles with these. The XML is going to see them as different because of the capitalization that comes with it, and it will start to treat this code as an erroneous syntax. In order to get this error fixed, you would have to change the ending tag so that it was lower case rather than the upper case that was used.

Another rule that you will need to keep track of when using your tags in XML is that you need to close them properly. For example, if you have a tag that is opened up inside of another element, you will need to make sure that it has been closed before the external element is all closed up.

When it comes to naming the tags that you will use, you need to be careful to get them the right way. For example, make sure that you are doing a good job of picking out the upper case and lower case letters and keeping them consistent when naming things is important. You also are not able to use any form of XML, regardless of the case that you are using, because it is going to confuse the processor and how it should behave. You can add in letters, digits, hyphens, underscores, and periods inside of the names of the elements. However, if you are using punctuation inside of this code, you are only able to use the underscore, hyphen, and period. The names of the elements are not able to have spaces. Outside of these simple rules, you are able to use any name that you would like to name the tags of your code.

Elements that are used in XML

Next on the list to explore are the elements that are inside of XML. The elements are kind of like the building blocks of the language, the part that is going to be built up on the foundation of the tags. These elements are great to work as containers that hold many things such as media objects, elements, attributes, and text and often they are going to hold many of these at once. Any of the documents that you work with inside of XML will have at least one of these elements, but the longer ones will hold more. For empty elements, the scopes will be delimited with the help of an empty element tag, but for the ones that have elements inside of them, the scopes are going to be delimited with the help of a start tag and an end tag.

Writing out the syntax of the element can be pretty easy, but here is a simple example to help you get it started:

<element-name attribute1 attribute2>

Whatever content you would like to add into here.

</element-name>

With the example above, the element name is going to be whatever name you would like to give the element in this case and then the attribute 1 and the attribute 2 are going to be the attributes that you give to your element, and they will be divided up with some white space. The attribute word is going to pretty much define the property of the element. It is going to work by associating the name back to the corresponding value, which is typically going to be a string of characters. When you would like to write out the attribute, you will simply write it out as name="value" and that is it.

When you are working on writing out the name of your element, take the time to see that the name you use in the start tag will be the same as the name that you place into the end tag. In addition, the word name should have an equal sign with it, as well as a string value that is inside of either double quotes or single quotes.

What about the empty element?

So above we were talking about a code that has an element inside of it. But there are times when you will have an empty element. Basically, the empty element is going to be an element that doesn't have content in it. When you are writing the syntax for this one, you would need to use the following format to tell the processor what to do:

If you are trying to create a new document and you will need to use a variety of elements, the following format is going to be the best:

```
<?xml version = "1.0"?>
<contact-information>
<address category = "home">
<name> Wendy Dawn </name>
<office> My Office </office>
<phone> (632) 246 1234 </phone>
<address/>
</contact-information>
```

Working with elements and tags inside of the XML document is one of the best things that you are able to do for your code. These are going to help you to get everything in place and they are the foundation and the building blocks that you really need inside of your code. It can take some time to learn the different things that you need inside of these, but when you are able to bring it all together, these are the two parts of the code that you need in order to really get it started the right way.

Chapter 7: Viewers and Editors in XML

Inside of XML, there are several methods that you are able to use in order to view documents. For example, you are able to use a browser in order to view a document, or you can choose to go with a simple text editor. Most of the browsers that are available will support XML, so this shouldn't be a worry. Or you can choose to just click on the files for XML and get them to open up; but remember that this is only going to work if the XML file is a local one. If the file is one that is found on your server, you just need to type in the right URL path into the address bar, just like when you want to open up some of the other files on your browser.

As mentioned, there are many ways that you are able to look and view the XML documents at any time that you would like and the method that you choose is going to be a personal decision. Some of the options include:

XML text editors: there are many text editors that you are able to use and you can make the decision that is right for you. Notepad, TextEdit, and Textpad are great options to work with to create and view documents in XML, but other options will work as well.

Google Chrome: while all browsers are going to work well with XML, this one is really good to work with. there seems to be few problems with using it and it makes it easy to open up the XML code you want to use.

Mozilla Firefox: this one is also a good browser to use, but you do need to first open the code in Google Chrome. To do this, you need to take the file and double click on it in order to see the code displayed in some colorful text. This is a good thing because it makes it easier to read the code. Then at the left portion of the element, you will see a plus and a minus sign. If you click on the plus sign, the code is going to expand but if you click on the minus sign, you will see that the code hides.

Errors in my document

There are times when there will be some errors in your XML documents. If you notice that the code is missing out on certain tags, there are some errors that are going to show up. If there is an error somewhere in the code, you are going to get a message that should contain some information about the error that you are

51

dealing with. sometimes it is something simple such as misspelling a word or using lower case in the start tag and then upper case in the end tag. You will need to double check your code to see what the issue is so that you can make some changes to the code.

Editors in XML

When you are working inside of XML, you are going to need to work with an editor of some sort. The editor is going to be useful to create, as well as make changes, in the document that you are using. There are many different editors that you are bale to use and most of them are free and may even come on your computer already, so this can make things easier. For example, Notepad or Wordpad are two great options that you can use, or you can download a professional editor to use from online. The online editors are a bit more powerful and sometimes beginners like to go with them because they do some of the work, such as close tags that you leave open, check the syntax, and highlight the syntax in color so that it is easier to read. You can make the decision about what kind you would like to use and the features that you think will be the most helpful when you are learning how to code.

Conclusion

Working with a new coding language is something that can take some time and effort. You want to be able to get the most out of the language, but you also don't want to waste your time on something that is too hard to learn and understand. This guidebook is going to take a bit of time to discuss the XML coding language, how to use it and why you would want to learn this particular language.

Inside this guidebook, you are going to learn everything you need in order to do well with the XML code. We are going to start out with some of the basics that come with XML coding, such as what it is and how it varies from HTML (even though both of them are pretty similar) and then move on to some of the special parts that are found inside of your first code so that you can become more familiar with it all. Then we move on how you would declare inside of XML (which is something that is optional and you can choose to do or not) along with working in comments and special characters' amount other topics.

There is so much that you are able to do with the XML code once you take the time to learn this code and what all you can do with it. When you are ready to get started in coding or you are looking for a new code that you can work with, make sure to take some time to look through this guidebook and get the most out of the XML code.

www.ingramcontent.com/pod-product-compliance
Lightning Source LLC
Chambersburg PA
CBHW070901070326
40690CB00009B/1945